NUCLEAR ENERGY

COLIN GRADY

Enslow Publishing

101 W. 23rd Street
Suite 240
New York, NY 10011
USA

enslow.com

Published in 2017 by Enslow Publishing, LLC.
101 W. 23rd Street, Suite 240, New York, NY 10011

Library of Congress Cataloging-in-Publication Data
Names: Grady, Colin, author.
Title: Nuclear energy / Colin Grady.
Description: New York, NY : Enslow Publishing, 2017. | Series: Saving the planet through green energy | Audience: Ages 8+. | Audience: Grades 4-6. | Includes bibliographical references and index.
Identifiers: LCCN 2016021787| ISBN 9780766082908 (library bound) | ISBN 9780766082885 (pbk.) | ISBN 9780766082892 (6-pack)
Subjects: LCSH: Nuclear energy—Juvenile literature. | Atoms—Juvenile literature. | Nuclear fission—Juvenile literature.
Classification: LCC QC792.5 .G73 2017 | DDC 333.792/4—dc23
LC record available at https://lccn.loc.gov/2016021787

Printed in China

To Our Readers: We have done our best to make sure all website addresses in this book were active and appropriate when we went to press. However, the author and the publisher have no control over and assume no liability for the material available on those websites or on any websites they may link to. Any comments or suggestions can be sent by e-mail to customerservice@enslow.com.

Portions of this book originally appeared in the book *Nuclear Energy: Amazing Atoms* by Amy S. Hansen.

CONTENTS

WORDS TO KNOW

accidents Unexpected and sometimes bad things that happen.

atoms The smallest parts of elements.

fossil fuel Fuel, such as coal, natural gas, or gasoline, that is made from plants that died millions of years ago.

generate To make.

generator A machine that makes electricity.

gravity The force that causes objects to move toward each other.

meltdown When the core of a nuclear power plant gets too hot and lets harmful energy escape.

microscopes Instruments used to see very small things.

nuclear force The force that holds the centers of atoms together.

nuclear reactor A machine in which nuclear power is safely created.

pellets Small, round things.

reactions Actions caused by things that have happened.

release To let go.

uranium A heavy metallic element that gives off rays of energy.

CHAPTER 1

WHAT IS NUCLEAR ENERGY?

Have you ever wondered what holds your house together? You may say it is nails or wood. And as all things are, nails and wood are made of **atoms**. But what holds atoms together? The nucleus, or center, of an atom is held together by something called the **nuclear force**. This force is strong. When something changes the nuclear force, atoms **release** lots of energy. This energy is called nuclear energy.

The sun's light and heat are forms of nuclear energy. They are released by nuclear **reactions** in the sun. On Earth, people capture nuclear energy by breaking **uranium** atoms apart. This reaction releases heat that we use to **generate** electricity.

A LOOK AT ATOMS

Atoms are too tiny to see, except with the best **microscopes**. However, atoms themselves are made up of even smaller things, called particles. These particles have energy. There are three kinds of particles, called protons, electrons, and neutrons. What

All the things you see around you—your house, a soccer ball, and you— are made of atoms.

Iron

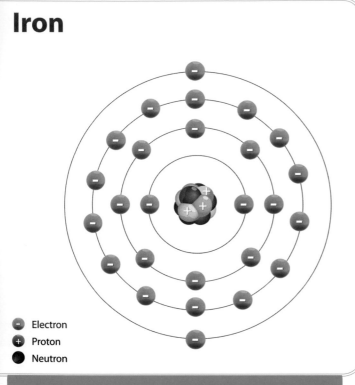

Electron
Proton
Neutron

The center of an atom is the nucleus. The nucleus of all atoms has protons and neutrons. An iron atom always has 26 protons.

kind of element an atom is depends on the number of protons it has. For example, iron always has 26 protons. Lead has 82 protons.

An atom's electrons circle around its nucleus. Protons and neutrons make up the nucleus. The protons and neutrons are held together by the nuclear force. Energy is released when these particles break apart or come together.

CHAPTER 2

NUCLEAR FUSION IN THE SUN

Our sun is about 93 million miles (150 million kilometers) away from Earth. But there is a reaction that happens there that gives our planet the energy we need for life. This reaction that releases nuclear energy in the sun is nuclear fusion. "Fusion" means putting smaller things together to make something larger.

HYDROGEN TO HELIUM

In the sun, two atoms of the element hydrogen fuse together to make one atom of the element helium. Hydrogen atoms have one proton, while helium atoms have two protons. This reaction releases lots of energy.

The crew of the International Space Station took this photo of the sun over Earth. Although the sun is 93 million miles (150 million km) away, it supplies all of the energy Earth needs for living things to grow.

The nuclear force holding together an atom's nucleus is so strong that it is hard to form or break. Atoms do not usually fuse together. However, the sun's center is very hot, and the **gravity** there is very strong. These conditions allow fusion to happen.

Nuclear fusion takes place at the center of the sun.

NUCLEAR ENERGY TIMELINE

1789   Martin Heinrich Klaproth discovers uranium.

1896   Henri Becquerel discovers radiation in uranium.

1902   Ernest Rutherford and Frederick Soddy suggest how radioactivity works.

1934   Enrico Fermi breaks apart an atom and causes nuclear fission.

1942–1945 During World War II, the United States secretly builds an atomic bomb. The bomb works. The war ends.

1957   The first big nuclear power plant in the United States starts running in Pennsylvania.

1973 US power companies start building 41 nuclear power plants, the most ever in one year.

1979 Three Mile Island nuclear power plant in Pennsylvania nearly has a partial **meltdown**. Safety changes begin.

1980 In the United States, more electricity is made from nuclear power than from oil for the first time.

1986 The Chernobyl nuclear power plant malfunctions. The core melts and radiation escapes.

2011 A tidal wave causes nuclear disaster at the nuclear power plant in Fukushima, Japan. Three cores melt and radiation escapes. Clean up could take up to forty years.

CHAPTER 3

NUCLEAR FISSION

How can scientists release the energy contained in an atom? The answer is nuclear fission. "Fission" means breaking apart. In nuclear fission, atoms are broken apart. People can make electricity with the energy released during nuclear fission. Scientists use certain uranium atoms for nuclear fission.

BREAKING URANIUM ATOMS

Uranium atoms are very large. These big atoms break apart more easily than smaller ones would. Scientists break up a uranium atom with tiny neutrons. When a neutron hits

NUCLEAR FISSION

the uranium atom, it breaks it into smaller atoms. This releases energy and frees other neutrons. The first neutron and the newly freed neutrons hit other uranium atoms. Those atoms break apart, too. Atoms continue to break apart and energy keeps being released.

People dig uranium out of the earth. The uranium is sent to places that make nuclear energy.

CHAPTER 4

USING FISSION TO MAKE ELECTRICITY

A **nuclear reactor** is a machine that can make electricity. It uses the heat energy given off during nuclear fission. The reactor collects this heat and changes it to electricity.

The reactor holds uranium **pellets**. One pellet is about the size of your fingertip. It holds as much energy as 150 gallons (568 liters) of oil. The pellets are put inside long metal rods and placed in a bundle, or core. The core is a small room with thick, solid walls. It is filled with cold water. The cold water helps cool the heat from the uranium core. Otherwise, the core can melt and lead to a meltdown.

Once the nuclear reaction starts, the rods send off heat. This boils the water. The boiled water or steam is pumped to a **generator** that uses its heat to make electricity.

This nuclear reactor core holds rods of uranium pellets. When the rods are used up, they are stored at the bottom of the pool of water.

NUCLEAR ENERGY IN HISTORY

Uranium is one of several elements whose atoms sometimes break apart naturally. Scientists noticed this over 100 years ago. They studied these elements and learned about the particles that make up atoms. For

The San Onofre Nuclear Power Plant in San Clemente, California, is one of more than 60 nuclear power plants in the United States. The plants are located near water, so that the water can be used to cool the reactors.

years, scientists tried to capture the energy that is released by uranium to make electricity.

After World War II started in 1939, many scientists tried to make bombs that used nuclear energy. In 1945, American scientists created the first nuclear bombs. The bombs helped end the war. Soon after, nuclear scientists started trying to make electricity again. The first American nuclear plant opened in 1957 in Shippingport, Pennsylvania.

CHAPTER 5

IS NUCLEAR ENERGY SAFE?

Nuclear power plants do not make as much air pollution as **fossil fuel** power plants do. But nuclear power is not perfect. When uranium is removed from the ground, the digging tears up land. Also, uranium is a nonrenewable energy source. This means that Earth's supply of uranium could get used up over time.

NUCLEAR WASTE

Another problem with nuclear power is nuclear waste. This is what is left over when uranium pellets will no longer work in a reactor. Nuclear waste leaks radiation, or energy that hurts living things. The waste must be stored